Write Your Lab Report

SUPER
QUICK
SKILLS

Write Your Lab Report

Diana Hopkins
Tom Reid

Los Angeles | London | New Delhi
Singapore | Washington DC | Melbourne

Los Angeles | London | New Delhi
Singapore | Washington DC | Melbourne

SAGE Publications Ltd
1 Oliver's Yard
55 City Road
London EC1Y 1SP

SAGE Publications Inc.
2455 Teller Road
Thousand Oaks, California 91320

SAGE Publications India Pvt Ltd
B 1/I 1 Mohan Cooperative Industrial Area
Mathura Road
New Delhi 110 044

SAGE Publications Asia-Pacific Pte Ltd
3 Church Street
#10-04 Samsung Hub
Singapore 049483

Editor: Jai Seaman
Editorial assistant: Lauren Jacobs
Production editor: Sarah Cooke
Marketing manager: Catherine Slinn
Cover design: Shaun Mercier
Typeset by: C&M Digitals (P) Ltd, Chennai, India

Library of Congress Control Number: 2019955163

British Library Cataloguing in Publication data

A catalogue record for this book is available
from the British Library

ISBN 978-1-5297-1898-0

Contents

Everything in
this book!

Section 1   What is a lab report for?

Find out why you are being asked to write a lab report. You will learn
what the reader needs to know and why they need to know it.

Section 2   What are the different sections in a lab report?

Here, the obligatory sections of a lab report and their purpose are
described, as well as the order they are presented in and what to
include.

Section 3   What different types of lab report are there?

You will see how lab reports in different subjects can have slight
variations (e.g. Engineering, Psychology, Pharmacology, or Physics).

Section 4   How do I start writing my lab report?

You will get advice on the steps you should take before, during and after
writing your lab report to avoid wasting time and getting confused.

Section 5   What style of writing do I use?

This section looks at the language used in lab reports, and identifies how the language can differ between different sections.

Section 6   What visuals can I use in my lab report?

Here you learn how to incorporate tables and figures into your work, and what you need to do to help the reader understand them.

Section 7   How and where do I refer to published work?

You will learn how (and why) to refer to theory and published research in the appropriate parts of your lab report.

Section 8   How much do I write?

You will learn about the relative lengths and balance of writing in the different sections.

Section 9   What is my tutor looking for?

This section uses typical university assessment criteria to show you what you need to do to get a good grade.

Section 10   How can I check I have done a good job?

Finally, you will be given tips to help you proof read and edit your work to ensure you submit the best piece of work you can.

What is a lab report for?

10 second
summary

Find out why you are being asked to write a lab report. You will learn what the reader needs to know and why they need to know it.

60 second summary

Why do we write lab reports?

Lab reports are a fundamental aspect of scientific research. We write lab reports so that:

- we have a clear document that someone else can use to carry out the same experiment again;

- we can demonstrate our understanding of the purpose of the experiment and the theoretical or historical background relating to that experiment;

- we can demonstrate to our tutor that we can write in a scientific style (concisely, accurately and clearly);

- we can develop our communication skills as preparation for writing longer research reports or academic papers.

The most important thing to remember when writing your lab reports is be clear, concise and accurate, and to follow the appropriate academic and scientific conventions.

A student told us

'I understood the theory better by actually doing the experiment, and then, when I had to write it up, I was able to explain the theory more clearly to myself, which was good preparation for later exams.'

Why are lab reports important?

Professional scientists write lab reports to document something important they have done. This then allows others to:

- evaluate their research methods and conclusions;

- try to replicate their results.

Lab report
A description and analysis of a laboratory experiment that investigates a scientific concept to facilitate scientific research.

A detailed lab report also allows the experimenters themselves to:

- look back at their work and assess strengths and weaknesses in their approach, materials and equipment;

- make improvements and/or changes in future research they do.

What other reasons are there for writing lab reports?

You will be writing lab reports as part of your course, and probably as an assessed assignment. Your lab report needs to be written clearly, accurately and in an appropriate academic and scientific style in order to get a good mark.

Your tutor wants to see if you have followed the lab instructions, and if you understand the purpose of the experiment. They also want to see if you can collect data, and explain what those data mean.

But good writing is not just about getting a good mark. Communicating science well is part of the scientific research process, and writing lab reports helps you to become a better scientist. This is because the skills you need in scientific inquiry, such as problem identification, problem solving, and drawing conclusions from evidence, are all sharpened and improved through clear thinking and effective communication.

Clear writing demonstrates clear thinking.

ACTIVITY

Do you understand the rationale behind writing lab reports?

Choose the best answer, A, B, or C, to the following questions.

1 Why has your tutor asked you to write a lab report?

   A   To check you have actually carried out the experiment.

   B   To provide practice in writing a scientific document.

   C   To find out who is the best student.

2 Why is it important to give details of methods and materials?

   A   To allow another person to carry out the same experiment.

   B   Because your tutor needs to know you followed the instructions in the lab manual.

   C   To avoid plagiarising your lab manual.

3 Which of the following reasons explain why professional scientists value well-written lab reports? You can choose more than one. Scientists value well-written lab reports because:

   A   clear writing is an indicator of clear thinking – an important characteristic for a scientist.

   B   it is important to be able to communicate your scientific work effectively.

   C   they are part of the process of carrying out scientific enquiry and can help lead to improving skills such as evaluating and problem solving.

Answers:

1 B

2 A

3 All of the answers are true.

A lab report is really just a scaled-down research paper. So learning how to write a really good lab report will set you up if you want to go on to do further research after you finish your university degree.

Getting your research published in a recognised, peer-reviewed journal is not easy, but you are more likely to be successful if the research you are describing is communicated effectively so that readers are clear about the message.

So being given the opportunity to develop these scientific communication skills whilst you are a student can help you later on and act as a stepping stone to your future career. Remember to use the feedback your tutor gives you to sharpen your scientific writing skills and to learn how to be the best communicator of research that you can.

Try scoring these statements on a scale of 0–5, where 0 is low agreement and 5 is high agreement.

Score

1   I am clear about the reasons behind writing lab reports. ☐

2   I think is important to take care with my
writing in my lab report. ☐

3   I understand how practising writing a lab report
can help me in my future career. ☐

4   I am confident that I can write a good
lab report. ☐

What are the different sections in a lab report?

10 second
summary

Here, the obligatory sections of a lab
report and their purpose are described,
as well as the order they are presented
in and what to include.

60 second summary

Getting to know the lab report sections

All lab reports are divided into logically ordered and clearly labelled sections, as described below. Each section has a different purpose, and includes enough information to fulfil that purpose. Even though some subjects may use slightly different labels for some of the sections, the purposes for the sections and the kind of information included are generally the same.

Before you write a lab report you need to know about the different sections and what sort of information you must include. That way you can keep appropriate records whilst doing your experiment, so you have everything you need when it comes to writing up the lab report.

The sections

Most 'typical' lab reports include sections with these headings, in the following order:

Typical lab report section headings

1   Abstract

2   Introduction

3   Method

4   Results

5   Discussion

6   Conclusion

7   References

Do be careful however. Some subjects and tutors may require you to use slightly different names for some of these sections. Always check with your tutor before you write your lab report. See Section 3 for more details.

Optional sections

Some lab reports may include other optional sections. Your tutor will inform you if you need to include these.

Possible optional sections (usually only required in longer reports):

• Contents page

• List of symbols

• List of tables and figures

• List of equations

• Appendices

The purpose of each section and what to include

Abstract

This provides a complete overview of the entire report. It is normally written as a single, short (often around 200 words) paragraph (but see the next chapter for variations in this style).

Abstract A brief summary (typically 150–250 words) of a research study which includes aims, methods used, results and overall conclusions.

An Abstract allows a busy reader to understand your aims, methods, results and conclusions quickly, so that they can decide whether they need to read the whole lab report (although for assessment purposes, your tutor *will* read your entire report!).

An Abstract should therefore include one or two concise sentences that describe each of the following:

- Your experimental aims and/or hypothesis.

- Theoretical information or previous research that led to your aims / hypothesis.

- The methods you used to carry out the experiment.

- Your key results or findings.

- The significance of your results (i.e. what they show or indicate and why this is important).

Note: the Abstract should be the last thing you write, as it is a summary of the whole report.

Summary An alternative term for Abstract (e.g. in engineering lab reports).

A student told us

Introduction

Your reader needs to know why the experiment is important. Start your Introduction with background information that sets the context of the experiment. This should answer the following question:

• What do we already know and how do we know it?

Whilst answering this question, it is likely that you will need to refer to your reading and cite your sources (see Section 7).

The next thing your reader wants to know is what you want to find out. This is your aim or your hypothesis. You should include the answer to this question:

• What is the purpose of this experiment?

To answer this question you will say something like:

The aim of this experiment is to …

This experiment aims to find out …

This experiment attempts to prove ...

Use your introduction like you would use a map. Look at the overall picture, decide where you want to go, why you want to go there, and then find the best route to get you there.

Method and Materials/Procedure/Experiment

Here you describe what *was done.* Your reader needs to find out *how* you carried out the experiment for two main reasons:

1   To be able to carry out the same experiment in exactly the same way again (i.e. to replicate the experiment).

2   To assess the validity of the conclusions you draw later in your report. In other words, have you explained how you took your measurements, how you ensured your results were reliable, how you tried to overcome possible errors etc.?

You need to include information about:

●   the steps carried out;

●   the equipment used (and you may need labelled diagrams of the experimental set-up

●   materials used and subjects involved (if appropriate).

A student told us

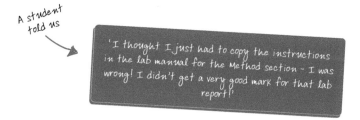

'I thought I just had to copy the instructions in the lab manual for the Method section – I was wrong! I didn't get a very good mark for that lab report!'

Results

Tell your reader what experimental results you have collected. This may include results of calculations and error analysis. You will probably also include figures and tables here.

Important points:

- Sometimes, if you have multiple results, you will need to divide this section using clear sub-headings.

- You don't need to include all the detailed data from your lab book (unless they need explanation), just the final, key results.

- Your reader needs to be able to understand your results so that they could, if they wanted, use them to draw their own conclusions, (as well as check that your conclusions are appropriate!).

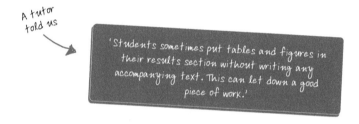

A tutor told us

'Students sometimes put tables and figures in their results section without writing any accompanying text. This can let down a good piece of work.'

Discussion

Here you should describe the significance of the numerical data from your Results section. Answer the following questions:

- What important things have you learnt from this experiment?

- Why are they important?

- What could be improved if you did it again? In other words, were there any errors, limitations, problems in the methods, materials, equipment or data analysis?

Conclusion

This section should remind the reader of the aims of the experiment (or hypothesis) and the results, with a clear statement of the significance of those results.

Don't include any new ideas or information in a Conclusion.

References

Here you list in full all the sources you have referred to in your lab report. You should follow the appropriate conventions for the referencing system you are using (see Section 7).

References The list of sources of information (from a textbook, an academic article etc. used in academic work.

ACTIVITY Can you recognise the section from the extracts?

Which section (a–e in the box below) do you think sentences 1–5 come from, and which words tell you?

1   Figure 3 shows a linear relationship and this suggests that further data could be extrapolated.

2   Boyle's Law will be used to predict the outcome of changing the volume on the initial state of a fixed quantity of gas.

3   There were some inaccuracies, which could have been due to the set-up of the equipment.

4   A fixed quantity of the unknown compound was tested initially.

5   The results supported the hypothesis.

a Introduction	c Results	e Conclusion
b Method	d Discussion	

Answers:

1 Results (words about data and referencing to Figure 3);

2 Introduction (reference to theory, and use of 'will' to explain the next step);

3 Discussion (words about errors and limitations);

4 Method (explaining what was done);

5 Conclusion (description of the success/outcome of the experiment)

Do you know what you need to include?

Does your lab report achieve the following:

1   Include a short Abstract that summarises the
    whole experiment?   ☐

2   Give sufficient background information in the Introduction? ☐

3   Allow another person to do the same experiment
    in exactly the same way?   ☐

4   Include clearly presented results (using words *and* tables
    and/or figures)?   ☐

5   Include a discussion of the original aims and the
    success or otherwise of the experiment?   ☐

6   Cite all sources accurately?   ☐

What different types of lab report are there?

10 second
summary

You will see how lab reports in
different subjects can have slight
variations (e.g. Engineering, Psychology,
Pharmacology, or Physics).

What different types of lab report are there?

Although all lab reports share a similar *purpose*, there can be some differences in style and organisation between different disciplines. This is because the *way* experiments are carried out varies enormously, and different types of information are therefore necessary in some lab reports but not in others. For example, in Pharmacology, Psychology, and the Social Sciences more generally, it may be necessary to give details of subjects/participants (e.g. animals, volunteers etc.), which would most likely not be the case in a physics lab report. In some lab reports, the different parts (described in Section 2) may be sub-divided (such as separate sections for Method, Materials/Equipment set-up), merged into single sections (such as Results and Discussion), or have different labels (such as Abstract/Summary).

Different types of lab report

Some subjects and tutors may require you to use slightly different names for some of the typical lab report sections. Always check with your tutor before you write your lab report. Common alternatives are shown in the table:

Typical lab report section headings	Possible alternative section headings	Notes	
Abstract	Summary	'Summary' is often used in *engineering* subjects	
Introduction	Background/ Theory	A *separate* 'Theory' section that lays out the theory on which the experiment is based, is sometimes included after the Introduction	
Method	Experimental/ Procedure/ Methods and materials	Sometimes there is a *separate section* for Materials or Equipment	
Results	Findings/Results and Analysis	Sometimes these two sections are *merged* into *Results and Discussion*	Sometimes these two sections are *merged* into *Discussion and Conclusions*
Discussion			
Conclusion	Conclusions		
References		This is typical across most disciplines	

A student told us

'I was glad I asked my tutor about the names of the sections, because it turned out she didn't want us to write a Conclusion section!'

Other variations

Some subjects, such as Pharmacy and Pharmacology, may wish you to divide your Abstract into very short paragraphs with sub-headings. Usually (but remember to check with your tutor) these sub-headings are:

- Aims

- Methods

- Results

- Conclusions

Subjects like Psychology, and Social Sciences, divide the Method section into separate parts with the following sub-headings:

Participants (this gives information about the subjects used in the experiment)

Materials (this describes equipment and test materials used)

Design (this explains the test design and the reason for its choice, and may include information about dependent and independent variables)

Procedure (this outlines what was done)

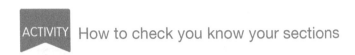

ACTIVITY How to check you know your sections

Try the following tasks:

1 Look at your lab report-marking criteria – do they suggest which section names to use?

2 Find a published research article (in a journal) about a topic of interest to you. Does it have different sections? What are they called?

3 Does your lab manual give advice on writing up your lab report, and which section names to use?

4 Are there specific instructions on your VLE that tell you how to organise your lab report?

Lab report and a technical report?

Sometimes, engineering departments may use the name technical report to refer to a lab report. However, more commonly, the term is used to refer to a longer report on a piece of research that may or may not take place in a laboratory. For example, a technical report may investigate and describe a design or a model, or it may review recent technological advances.

Technical report
A research document that describes the process, progress, or results of a technical or scientific study or analysis of a research problem. A technical report is typically longer and more in depth than a lab report.

CHECK POINT — Test what you know

What alternative names are there for the section called 'Abstract'?

....

....

Which sections are sometimes joined to form a single section?

....

....

What sub-headings might you find in the Method Section?

....

....

> Fear of the unknown is the greatest fear, so make it your business to know!

Congratulations

You've thought about why we write lab reports and what the different sections do. Now it's time to get writing!

How do I start writing my lab report?

10 second
summary

You will get advice on the steps you should take before, during and after writing your lab report to avoid wasting time and getting confused.

How do I get writing?

There are clear steps that you need to follow if you want to be as effective as possible when writing your lab report. Before you start writing, you need to gather together your lab book (notes from the lab experiment), your lab instruction manual, your reading, and your handbook with instructions on how to write up your lab. Only when you have familiarised yourself with the task, and have collected into one place all the documents you need, should you start planning your writing.

You then need to plan the sections and write an outline. You don't need to write the sections in the order they appear in the lab report. If you like, you can start with the Method/Procedure section, as this is often the easiest section to write.

The process of writing your lab report

For your lab report there are some clear steps you can follow to make the process easier and to help you get organised and started.

Use the flowchart opposite to help guide you through the writing up process.

Ten steps to writing your lab report

First steps:

Step 1

Gather all necessary documents and information together. Make sure you understand the instructions. Read the literature that allows you to write about the *background*.

Step 2

Plan your outline. Write notes under each section heading to indicate what you will include in the section.

Step 3

If you haven't already, now is the time to carry out your analysis of data or results, ready to start writing.

The next steps: getting writing

Step 4

Choose the section you find easiest to write (DO NOT start with the Abstract!).

Step 5

Start writing your first draft of your chosen section (using your outline as a guide, and following instructions carefully). This is likely to be *either* the Introduction, Method, or Results.

Step 6

Now write the remaining two easiest sections (see Step 5).

Step 9

Read your work to proof read and edit. Check that you have included not only clear information, but also that you have not 'waffled on'. Check for spelling and grammar mistakes.

Step 8

Once you have finished your first draft, walk away for a few hours, or if possible, a few days.

Step 7

Carefully read your Introduction and look at the analysis of your results. This will help you to identify the *significance* of your findings and allow you to start writing your Discussion (and then Conclusion).

Step 10

Check the instructions, the assessment criteria and your work one more time, to make sure you have done what you were asked.

A student
told us

'I wrote notes for each section first, and didn't start writing the full document until I had decided what I needed to say in each section.'

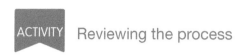

ACTIVITY Reviewing the process

Answer the following questions to check that you are prepared to start your report.

1   What documents do you need to check *before* you start writing?

....

....

2   Why should you do some reading of published literature *before* you start writing?

....

....

3   When you are ready to start writing, which sections are good ones to start with? Why?

....

....

4   Which section should you write last? Why?

....

....

5   What might you edit when you proof read?

....

....

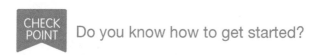

Try scoring these statements on a scale of 0–5, where 0 is low agreement and 5 is high agreement.

Score

1   I find it hard to start writing.   ☐

2   I have got all the information I need to write up
    my lab report.   ☐

3   I have decided what I will do first.   ☐

4   I have a plan for how to write my lab report.   ☐

What style of writing do I use?

10 second summary

This section looks at the language used in lab reports, and identifies how it can differ between the various sections.

60 second
summary

What style of writing do I use?

A lab report is a piece of academic writing, and therefore you need to use an academic style. It is also a piece of scientific writing, so you need to know the conventions of scientific writing too, such as how to write units of measurement, abbreviations, and use of the passive etc. Although the different sections of a lab report all follow an appropriate scientific style, there are some differences between them that are important to know.

For example, in the Introduction you use your reading to show that you understand the background, using a mix of tenses. In the Method section, however, you describe *what was done* using past tenses, and in the Discussion section, you will be likely to use present tenses to show the significance of your results or investigation.

Why does style matter?

All academic writing needs to be easy to understand, expressed accurately using correct grammar, spelling, punctuation, and vocabulary, and must follow conventions related to the specific type of writing used.

A lab report is a scientific document. It is essential that the message conveyed is clear and accurate. This is because one of the aims of a lab report is to allow someone else to carry out the same experiment in exactly the same way in order to replicate your results. Imagine if your writing was ambiguous and, for example, the quantities of materials used was unclear. Someone trying to replicate your experiment would not only certainly fail to achieve the same results as you, but it could also lead to unexpected and potentially unsafe outcomes.

A student told us

'I'm not sure if I am meant to explain the method as a series of instructions.'

What conventions do I need to know?

Abbreviations

Standard accepted abbreviations can be used in your lab report. These include the following:

- Units (e.g. mm, K, N, kg, ml, °C).

- Chemical compound symbols (e.g. CO_2, C_2H_5OH).

> **Abbreviation**
> A short form of a word or phrase used to replace the long form.

- Other accepted abbreviations such as e.g. and i.e., although these should only be used inside either brackets or commas, for example (*An inferential statistical test, e.g. Wilcoxon signed ranks test, or Chi-square test, can be used to analyse data.*).

Usually, however, you need to define abbreviations on first use, before using throughout your report. For example:

- To determine the aerobic endurance of the participants, maximum oxygen uptake (VO_2max) was measured during …

- … this involves a series of chemical reactions and is known as the citric acid cycle (CAC).

- The insulation of cables can be tested in a variety of ways including very low frequency (VLF), and time-domain eflectometry (TDR).

Note, however, that you should not use an abbreviation if you only use the term on one single occasion. Abbreviations are a way of using shorthand for frequently-used terms, so if a term is not used frequently, don't abbreviate it!

ACTIVITY What abbreviations are common in your subject?

1   List some of the most common abbreviations from your subject
     that you expect to be using in your writing.

     ....
     ....
     ....
     ....
     ....
     ....
     ....
     ....
     ....

2   Are any of these 'common knowledge', i.e. so common that you
     don't need to define the abbreviation (e.g. DNA in Biology – this
     is common knowledge because even non-biologists know what it
     means).

     ....
     ....
     ....
     ....
     ....
     ....
     ....
     ....
     ....

'I don't know if I should use long, technical words rather than more simple vocabulary in order to sound more academic.'

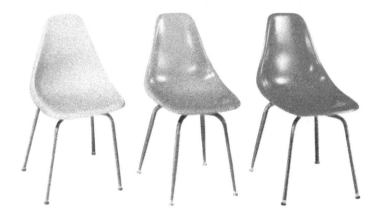

Formal language style

There are rules about formal style that you need to know:

Things to avoid 👎
Don't use contractions like *isn't, wasn't, can't* or *it's* in your lab report. ✕
Don't use informal two-word verbs such as *carry on, carry out, look into, put on, work out.* ✕
For numbers under ten (some style guides say twenty), don't use the numeral: *The experiment was repeated 5 times with 5 different conditions applied.* ✕
Don't start sentences with numerals: *21% of the participants were under 30.* *25 mg of the unknown compound was added to the solution* ✕
Don't use *vague* statements: *Appropriate equipment was used to measure maximum oxygen uptake.* *The load was increased a little, every so often.* ✕
Don't use subjective language: *The experiment was very successful.* ✕
Don't use unnecessarily long and technical words when there are more easily understood words and phrases: *The repositioning of the experimental set-up, effected an amelioration in the exactness of the results.* ✕

What to do instead 👍
Use full versions of the word groups, i.e. *is not, was not, cannot, it is.* ✓
Use single word, more formal equivalents such as *continue, perform/ conduct, investigate, place, calculate.* ✓
Write numbers under ten (or sometimes, twenty) as words: *The experiment was repeated five times with five different conditions applied.* ✓
If it is a percentage, write it in words: *Twenty one percent of the participants were under 30.* For other numbers, try to rearrange your sentence: *The unknown compound (25 mg) was added to the solution.* ✓
Be precise, with specific details: *A specially calibrated exercise cycle was used to measure maximum oxygen uptake, as shown in Figure 1.* *The load was increased in 1 kg increments every three minutes.*
Use objective language: *The aims of the experiment were achieved.* ✓
Only use technical words when absolutely necessary and never use rare, unusual words when there is a simple (but formal) alternative: *By rearranging the experimental set-up, the accuracy of the results was improved.* ✓

Using an objective style

Scientific writing tends to be impersonal and *objective*. This is because you are writing about facts and processes that are based on evidence. Scientific enquiry should not be subjective, open to interpretation, or based on our personal thoughts or beliefs.

In the Method section of your lab report you should ensure an objective style by avoiding use of words like *I, we, my, our* etc. This means that we are likely to use the passive construction when describing *what was done*.

Objective style
Fact/evidence-based and unbiased presentation of information and ideas (usually avoiding the use of personal pronouns like 'I' or 'we').

Passive construction
A type of grammar construction that describes 'what was done' rather than 'who did it'. In the case of scientific writing, for example, the experiment is more important than the experimenter.

Example 1:

Not (usually) appropriate: We measured the voltage drop across five different resistors.

Appropriate: The voltage drop *was measured* across five different resistors.

Example 2:

Not (usually) appropriate: I gave all the participants a consent form to sign.

Appropriate: All participants *were given* a consent form to sign.

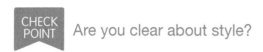

CHECK POINT — Are you clear about style?

Test your knowledge by answering the following questions:

	Yes or No?	What are they?
1 Do you know which abbreviations are standard in your field?		
2 Do you know the rules for using non-standard abbreviations?		
3 Are you clear about which kinds of words and phrases are too informal for a lab report?		
4 Do you know the rules about using numbers?		

Congratulations

You know how to start writing your lab report using an appropriate scientific style.

Now you can think about how to incorporate visuals and sources into your work.

What visuals can I use in my lab report?

10 second
summary

Here you learn how to incorporate tables and figures into your work, and what you need to do to help the reader understand them.

60 second
summary

Different kinds of visual information

A lab report can often include quite complex information. To help make this complex information easier to understand, we can use supporting visuals to represent the same information in a different format.

Visuals not only allow your reader to access information more easily, they can also help to make your lab report more interesting and professional. Your visuals can take a range of different forms. They can be graphs, diagrams, photographs, drawings, charts, or tables. These figures or tables are always accompanied by a clear title (caption or legend).

There are some simple conventions you need to follow when including this visual material in your lab report, such as how to label it, where to put the title, how to refer the reader to it, and where to place it in your text.

Using tables and figures

What is a table?

Tables are for data or other information, presented in columns and rows.

Table 3 Sources, pathways and receptors of heavy metals discovered in Area X

	Inorganic sources	Pathway a Inhalation b Ingestion c Dermal contact	Effect on receptor
Arsenic (As)	Mining, wood treatment, paints and pigments, ammunition, textiles, glass, biosolids (historic: pesticides)	a. atmospheric transfer b contaminated groundwater c. dust	Corrosive to gastrointestinal tract, damaging to vital organs incl. skin, respiratory effects, carcinogenic
Cadmium (Cd)	Mining, paints and pigments, nickel–cadmium batteries, plastics, electronics	a. atmospheric transfer	Toxic to kidney and respiratory system, carcinogen
Copper (Cu)	Pesticides, biosolids, electrical equipment	a. atmospheric transfer b. contaminated food and drink c. dust	Metal fume fever, nausea, skin inflammation Damages plant root growth
Lead (Pb)	Mining, batteries, pesticides, biosolids, coal, ash, ammunition (historic: petrol, paint, plumbing)	a. atmospheric transfer b. contaminated food, drink, soil	Toxic to all systems of body, especially neurological system
Nickel (Ni)	Biosolids, stainless steel industry, electrical equipment, jewellery, nickel–cadmium batteries	a. contaminated food b. jewellery, coins	Nausea, skin irritation, asthma Slows plant growth and metabolism
Zinc (Zn)	Pesticides, biosolids, mining	a. atmospheric transfer b. contaminated food c. dust	Metal fume fever Disrupts plant root tip cells

(Chin, 1995; UK Government, 2013; WHO, 2012; Sheldon & Menzies, 2004; Ahmad & Ashraf, 2011; Rout & Das, 2009)

Table 4 Estimated time in the park, distance walked and percentage area covered by each receptor

	Length of time spent in park (minutes)	Path length (miles)	Assumed area coverage on path (%)	Assumed area coverage (%)
Dog walkers	60	2.50	1.5	2
Leisure walkers	30	1.25	0.5	1
Family having a picnic	180	..	..	6
Education groups	180	1.00	0.5	6
Park rangers	360	15.0	7.0	12
Regular volunteers	180	7.5	3.5	6

'I'm not sure if I can use graphs and pie charts for my data presentation instead of writing words.'

What is a figure?

Figures are any visual representations of information that is not a table. So this means your graphs, bar charts, diagrams, schematics, and images are all titled Figures in a lab report.

- Graphs and charts present data.

- Images, diagrams and schematics demonstrate models, equipment set-ups, chemical structures, or represent theories.

Table A set of facts or figures arranged systematically and usually displayed in rows and columns, often numbered, and found in academic texts such as lab reports and used to describe (often) complex information in a visual way.

Figure A picture, diagram or drawing, often numbered, found in academic texts such as lab reports and used to describe (often) complex information in a visual way.

Two ways of saying the same thing? What's not to like?

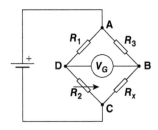

Figure 1 Schematic drawing of a Wheatstone bridge (Permission for use granted under the terms of the GNU Free Documentation License)

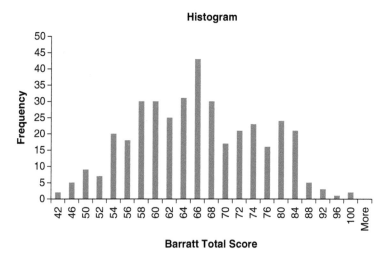

Figure 2 Frequency of scores on the Barrett test

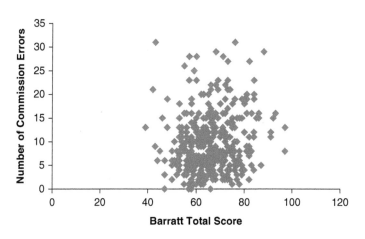

Figure 3 Commission errors

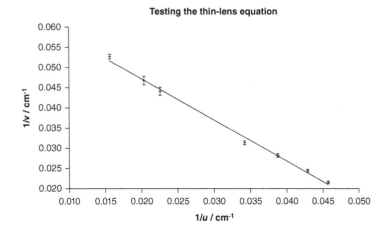

Figure 4 Graph of values 1/v against 1/u as calculated by the thin-lens equation from data Table 2

When do I use them?

Tables and figures are often used in the following sections:

- In the Introduction, when providing relevant information from a source to help clarify the background to the experiment.

- In the Method section to show experimental set-up or provide information about equipment.

- In the Results section to present your data in an easy-to-understand format.

- Sometimes, in the Discussion section to show concepts or theories that can be interpreted from the data/findings of your experiment.

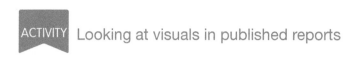

ACTIVITY Looking at visuals in published reports

Find an academic paper on a subject you are interested in.

Now:

1   Find the tables and figures.

2   Identify in which part of the paper they are used. Is it in all sections, or only in one or two sections (which ones?)?

3   Identify the *purpose* of the tables and figures.

4   Find out how the reader is directed to them in the written text.

5   Identify what kind of information is included in these visuals.

Paper An academic article, but also sometimes can refer to a presentation delivered at a conference or symposium, and later written up for publication.

How do we label them?

All tables and figures need to have clear labels and a concise, relevant title (or caption or legend). The labels are for *inside* the table or figure. Titles for tables are placed *above* the table. Titles for figures are placed *below* the figure. Titles need numbers, with a different sequence for the tables and figures (e.g. Table 1 for the first table mentioned, and Figure 1 for the first figure mentioned). The words 'Table' and 'Figure' need a capital letter.

Labelling tables and figures

Tables

Rows and columns need headings to explain their contents following the rules shown below:

Title above the table

Columns labelled and units given

Table 1   Calibration data of lenses, aperture cradle and screen

	Rider position (cm)	*Correction (cm)*
Apertures	50.0	0.0
Screen	51.3	-1.3
150mm - lens	50.4	-0.4
300mm - lens	50.7	-0.7
150mm - lens optic centre	50.1	-0.1
300mm - lens optic centre	50.5	-0.5

Rows labelled

Numbers aligned correctly (**not** centred) and to consistent numbers after the decimal point

Figures

- Graphs and charts: provide clear labels on the axes.

- Pie charts and other graphics of quantity: provide a key.

- Diagrams and schematics: label all the parts.

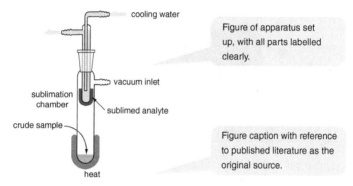

Figure of apparatus set up, with all parts labelled clearly.

Figure caption with reference to published literature as the original source.

Figure 1   Set up for vacuum sublimation purification [1].

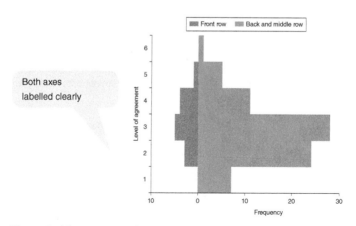

Both axes labelled clearly

Figure 1   Histogram showing conformity of responses to question 5 on questionnaire for different seating locations

Note that for any tables or figures that you have taken from an external source (i.e. you did not make them yourself), you need to provide a reference, just as you would any other information you have used that is not your own work.

A student told us

'I'm a bit unclear about the rules for using tables and figures.'

What do we need to include in the written part?

Remember that tables and figures are there to support your written explanations. They should *never* appear without being referred to in your writing. Use expressions like the following to direct your reader to the relevant visual information:

- Table 1 shows the uncertainties associated with these measurements.

- There are some uncertainties associated with these measurements (Table 1).

- The uncertainties associated with these measurements are shown in Table 1.

- As shown in Table 1, there are some uncertainties in these measurements.

Where do we put the visuals?

Your tables and figures need to be placed as close as possible to the part of the written text where they are mentioned. The reader should not have to scroll down to find them.

Ready to use tables and figures?

How confident are you with the rules for using tables and figures? Tick the statements that are true for you. If you are still not sure, go back and read the relevant section again.

1 I understand the reason for using tables and figures in my lab report. ☐

2 I know the difference between a table and a figure. ☐

3 I know which sections are most likely to include tables and figures. ☐

4 I can label my tables and figures correctly. ☐

5 I know that I need to make reference to the tables and figures in my accompanying written text. ☐

6 I understand that I need to place the tables and figures near to the part of the written text that refers to them. ☐

How and where do I refer to published work?

10 second
summary

You need to have a solid grasp of your subject area. Here you will learn how (and why) to refer to theory and published research in the appropriate parts of your lab report.

60 second summary

What do I need to know to make sure I reference correctly?

Before you write your lab report, you need to have good background knowledge about the theories upon which your own experiment is grounded and what research has already been done. To do this, you need to read extensively on the subject. You will then draw on this reading to provide, in your own words, background information that helps the reader contextualise your experiment and understand the reason for your investigation.

Every time you use information from your reading, you need to acknowledge where you found it. The original 'source' can be a book, a journal article, a paper written up in conference proceedings, or some other kind of scholarly literature.

There are clear rules about how to 'cite' these sources in your work, as well as how to build the list of references at the end.

> How can we build a future if we don't first find out about the past?

Why is it important to cite sources in my lab report?

We use other people's work to:

- give strength to our ideas;

- give evidence to support what we say;

- demonstrate that we are well-informed.

Every time we use someone else's work, we need to cite the source, so that:

- we give credit to the authors;

- someone else can easily find the same source;

- we avoid being accused of plagiarism;

- we show that we are following academic writing conventions.

A student told us

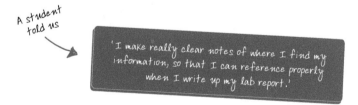

'I make really clear notes of where I find my information, so that I can reference properly when I write up my lab report.'

What rules do I need to know in order to avoid plagiarism?

OK, so we know that every time we use information from a source, we need to acknowledge it. But what else do we need to do?

You need to follow these rules:

1   Use your own words to talk about the information from the source. We call this 'paraphrasing', and it demonstrates that we understand the point clearly. Then provide a citation to show that the ideas are not yours.

2   If we do not change the words, we need to use quotation marks to show that it is a direct quote from the original source. However, direct quotations are *not common* in lab reports. Only use direct quotes if the specific word or phrase is controversial, or associated specificially with a particular person or group, or is impossible to write in your own words. With direct quotations, we need to provide page numbers in our in-text citation when using a name/date system.

Citation A quote from or reference to an academic or other formal text using a particular referencing system such as Harvard (name, date) or Vancouver (numeric).

Which sections will I cite sources in?

The Introduction

In this section you are providing the background for your experiment or research. This means you are likely to draw on published literature in order to build up the historical context (i.e. to show what is known already and where in the research your experiment sits).

Literature published books, journals and other academic texts on a specific subject or topic.

The Method

If you are using an established method or model or experimental technique, you will need to provide a reference.

> Example 1 from a biology lab report: The method used was a modified version of the Biuret Test, known as the BCA assay (Smith, 1985).

Also in this section, you may discuss your data collection and/or analysis methods, and make reference to the source from which you learnt about the method.

> Example 2 from a psychology lab report: The Barratt questionnaire denotes the Barratt Impulsivity Scale (Patton et al., 1995) which measures motor, attentional and non-planning impulsivity.

How do I know what system of referencing to use?

There are many different referencing systems, with different departments often using different systems. Even within the same department you may find different tutors having different preferences.

The most commonly used referencing systems are either *name and date* systems or *numerical* systems.

Name and date systems are where the authors are named and the date given, with the final reference list at the end of the lab report in alphabetical order. They include: Harvard, APA (American Psychological Association) *and* MLA (Modern Language Association).

Numeric systems use numbers in the text, with the final reference list organised numerically in the order they occurred in the lab report. They include: RSC (Royal Society of Chemistry), IEEE (Institute of Electrical and Electronic Engineers), IOP (Institute of Physics), and Vancouver systems.

When citing a source for the second time (and thereafter), use the same number used initially.

Ask your tutor which referencing system they wish you to use in your lab report.

What does an in-text citation look like?

Name and date in-text citations

APA	Harvard type
Type A personality can be defined as aggressive, dominating and goal-orientated (Friedman & Rosenman, 1974).	Type A personality can be defined as aggressive, dominating and goal-orientated (Friedman and Rosenman, 1974).
According to Friedman and Rosenman, (1974), Type A personality can be defined as aggressive, dominating and goal-orientated.	According to Friedman and Rosenman, (1974), Type A personality can be defined as aggressive, dominating and goal-orientated.

Numeric in-text citations

RSC	Vancouver type
Methods of detection for arsenic can be extremely sensitive.[1]	Methods of detection for arsenic can be extremely sensitive (1).
Lace et al[1] show that detection for arsenic can be extremely sensitive.	Lace et al (1) show that detection for arsenic can be extremely sensitive.

What does the list of references at the end look like?

Name and date reference list

APA	Harvard type
Friedman, M. & Rosenman, R. H. (1974). *Type A Behaviour and your Heart*. New York: Fawcett.	Friedman, M. and Rosenman, R.H., 1974. *Type A Behaviour and your Heart*. New York: Fawcett.

Numeric reference list

RSC	Vancouver type
A. Lace, D. Ryan, M. Bowkett and J. Cleary, *Molecules*, 2019, **24**, 339	Lace A, Ryan D, Bowkett M, Cleary J. Molecules. MDPI; 2019. **24**, 339p

Where can you get help with referencing?

Your university or college library will have clear guidance on how to cite sources, both in-text and when producing your reference list at the end of your work.

> **Referencing**
> A particular system such as Harvard, APA or Vancouver to refer to a source in academic work, which includes information that tells the reader where the source came from.

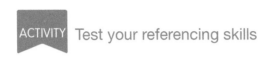

ACTIVITY Test your referencing skills

Imagine you are a psychology student and you have just read two useful articles on the subject of your experiment. You have made the following notes (in your own words) from each paper:

Paper 1: Cherry, E.C. (1953) 'Some experiments on the recognition of speech, with one and two ears', *Journal of the Acoustical Society of America,* 25, 975–979.

Notes: When there is a lot of conversation going on around us, we are generally only able to focus on one voice at a time. However, the research has some possible problems in methodology.

Paper 2: Wood, N. and Cowan, N. (1995) 'The Cocktail Party phenomenon revisited: How frequent are attention shifts to one's name in an irrelevant auditory channel?', *Journal of experimental psychology: Learning Memory and Cognition,* 21 (1): 225–260.

Notes: Participants were tested with how well they responded to hearing their name from a source that was not the one they were concentrating on. People with good working memories can focus their attention on external input more easily than those with poor working memory capacity (WMC).

Now look at the way the student has used this information in their lab report Introduction. What problems are there? Jot your thoughts down, and have a go at rewriting the segment.

Early research which suggested that we are only able to focus on one voice when we are in an environment with a lot of voices talking at once (such as a cocktail party) was limited by some problems with its methodology. However, more recent research has confirmed these original findings and, moreover, has shown that the people most likely to find it hard to attend to external input had poor working memory capacity (WMC).

Feedback: The student has failed to cite their sources. They have successfully paraphrased from the original source, but this would still constitute plagiarism, as the ideas are not their own. They needed to write it something more like this:

Early research discussed by Cherry (1953) suggested that we are only able to focus on one voice when we are in an environment with a lot of voices talking at once (such as a cocktail party). However, this research was limited by some problems with its methodology (Wood & Cowan, 1995). More recent research has confirmed these original findings and, more-over, has shown that the people most likely to find it hard to attend to external input had poor working memory capacity (WMC) (Wood & Cowan, 1995).

....

....

....

....

....

CHECK POINT Are you clear about referencing systems?

Do you know the answers to the following questions for your subject?

1   Which referencing system do you need to use?   ☐

2   How are the sources cited in an in-text reference?   ☐

3   What does the list of references at the end look
     like in this system?   ☐

4   Where can I find more help to make sure I get it right?   ☐

Congratulations

You understand the importance of using visuals and citations, and you know the conventions you need to follow when using them.

Now it's time to make sure you have done a good job, by following your instructions, writing the right amount, and meeting the marking criteria.

How much do I write?

10 second
summary

Balance is key. Here you will learn
about the relative lengths and balance
of writing in different sections of your
report.

Writing the right amount

The quality of a lab report is not determined by its length. Lab reports can vary in size, depending on the experiment or research being documented, and the purpose of the lab report. However, whatever the length of your lab report, there needs to be a balance between the sections.

For some sections there are standard expectations of length in proportion to the overall length. For example, the Abstract is expected to be a short, concise, summary of the content of the whole lab report. This can be as short as 150 and usually no more than 250 words. In a similar way, the Conclusion should also be short, usually no more than 10–15% of the whole report.

The important thing to do is to make sure you have a balanced report.

'There's an old saying in Hollywood: It's not the length of your film, it's how you use it.'

↳ Ben Stiller

A student told us

'I don't know how long each section should be.'

The Title and Abstract

There are general rules of thumb for titles and abstracts, regardless of the overall length of the lab report. Remember, though, that these are generalisations which may differ depending on your assignment.

The Title

This tells the reader the purpose of the experiment and should be concise. Usually, a lab report title is no more than ten to fifteen words.

Tip!

Have a key word as close to the beginning of the title as possible.

Example title 1: An investigation into mechanical behaviour under load of four different specimen materials

Example title 2: A comparative evaluation of three different methods of testing personality

The Abstract

This summarises the entire experiment, including results and their significance. It is intended as a paragraph (or series of sentences) that will give a reader a quick overview of the report. It is generally considered possible to summarise a lab report in about 200 words, and most guidelines suggest a length of between 150 and 250 words.

Which sections are the longest and why?

There are no fixed rules about which sections are the longest. This very much depends on the actual experiment and the kind of report you are writing. You will probably be given guidelines and instructions from your tutor. However, if you are not given instructions about length, there are some general rules of thumb that can *serve as guidelines only.*

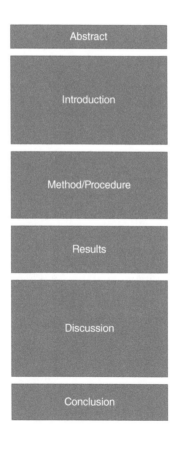

Figure 8.1

Abstract	The *Introduction* is a very important section,
Introduction	as you provide the reader with the background
	information necessary to understand the
	rationale for the experiment. If you are
	explaining complex theory, this section may
	take up a larger proportion of the lab report.
	The *Method* section can vary from very short
Method/Procedure	and straightforward to a much longer section,
	with descriptions of apparatus, procedure, data
	collection methods, and data analysis methods.
	The length of this section depends very much
	on the complexity and number of stages to the
	experiment(s).
	Results will (most likely) be a combination of
Results	written words and tables and figures. For a
	short report, the written words are likely to be
	brief, although there may still be a significant
	number of visual representations of the results.
Discussion	The most important section is your *Discussion.*
	This is where you explain your results, make
	inferences, and suggest the significance and
	importance of your results. In this section, you
	are probably going to refer back to published
	literature and give clear evidence for the
	implications of your results. Thus, this section is
	likely to take up a good proportion of your report.
Conclusion	Your *Conclusion* summarises the outcomes of
	the experiment, reinforces the significance of your
	results, and confirms whether your aims and/or
	your hypothesis has been fulfilled (or otherwise).

Figure 8.2   Approximate proportions for the different sections of a 'typical' lab report

What shall I do if there are no instructions about length?

If you are not given guidance, you should consider the following questions to help you decide how much to write:

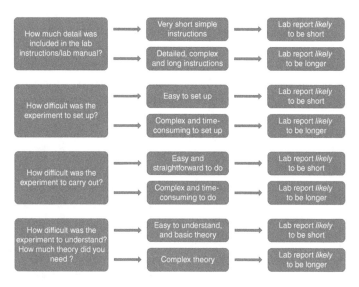

Figure 8.3 Helpful questions to determine possible length of your lab report

How do I check I have written enough?

The test of whether a lab report is successful or not is if:

(a) there is sufficient detail and information for someone else to replicate the experiment;

(b) there is sufficient evidence for the inferences made in the Discussion section, and the conclusions drawn to be valid.

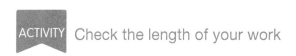

ACTIVITY Check the length of your work

To check that you have written enough, look back at the first draft of your report and answer these questions section by section:

1   Does the Introduction provide enough information on the historical and theoretical background that underpins the experiment(s)?

2   Does the Introduction draw on published literature when discussing the background?

3   Does the Introduction include the hypothesis and objective of the experiment?

4   Could someone else follow the steps given in the Method section, and be able to carry out the same experiment(s), with the same equipment?

5   Could someone else understand the data collection and data analysis methods used sufficiently to replicate them?

6   Are the results explained clearly in words and supported with appropriately labelled tables and figures?

7   Are the results presented and described sufficiently to allow a reader to draw the same conclusions you have drawn?

8   Does your Discussion section explain the significance of your results and link your findings to the objective set out in your Introduction?

9   Does the Discussion link back to published literature?

10   Have you discussed any possible limitations and errors in your Discussion?

11   Does the Conclusion summarise the signficance of the results?

And finally…

12   Does the Abstract summarise *the whole experiment, including results and achievement of the objective?*

How can I cut my writing if I have written too much?

Use the same checklist above, but this time, look at the parts of your sections that do *not* answer the questions to decide if:

- there are any parts that are superfluous, or irrelevant;

- you have included unnecessary details;

- you have repeated yourself unnecessarily within or between the different sections.

If, after these checks, your lab report is still too long, try to find sentences that can be made more concise through more careful use of language. For example:

This long sentence that includes unnecessary information:

> To set this practical up, first all the lights in the room were switched off and the subject was left for three minutes to dark-adapt in the room.

can be reworked to be more concise:

> First, the lights were switched off and the subject was left for three minutes to dark-adapt.

or this sentence:

> A short length of glass tubing was inserted into a stopper which was connected to one end of a plastic tube.

can be reworked to be more concise:

> A short length of glass tubing was inserted into a stopper connected to one end of a plastic tube.

A student told us

'My sentences always seem to end up too long. How do I cut them?'

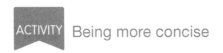

Have a go at rewriting these sentences to make them more concise:

1   The experimenter repeated each reading to ensure the experimenter was getting consistent results.

2   Here simple apparatus are chosen to the end of a quick and easy demonstration and quantification using commonly available apparatus of: solenoids, operational amplifiers and oscilloscopes.

> **Apparatus** The technical and/or laboratory equipment used to conduct an activity or experiment.

3   A divergence angle of 8.44° was found for the lower edge of the jet and 10.31° for the upper edge.

1 Each reading was repeated to ensure consistent results were obtained.

2 A simple apparatus consisting of solenoids, operational amplifiers and oscilloscopes allows a quick and easy demonstration and quantification.

3 Divergence angles of 8.14° o (lower edge of jet) and 10.31° o (upper edge) were found.

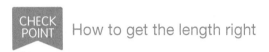

CHECK POINT — How to get the length right

Check that you are clear about the length of your lab report by answering the questions below.

	Yes or No?	What are they?
1 Do you know which sections have standard guidelines on length?		
2 Have you been given clear instructions about the length of your own lab report?		
3 Are you clear about the relative lengths of the different sections?		
4 Do you know how to check you have written sufficient information for your reader?		
5 Do you have strategies for cutting your work if it is too long?		

What is my tutor looking for?

10 second
summary

This section uses typical university assessment criteria to show you what you need to do to get a good grade.

Meeting the marking criteria

When your tutor marks your lab report they will be assessing how successfully you have fulfilled the task. To do this they will most likely use standardised marking criteria.

Most criteria not only judge the depth of your understanding and knowledge of the topic being investigated, but also assess the quality of your scientific writing. This means that you can gain or lose marks depending on how clearly you communicate your message, how successfully you adopt an appropriate scientific writing style, and how accurate your grammar, punctuation and spelling are.

You can generally gain a significant number of marks just by spending time proof reading and editing your work to ensure you meet the criteria related to effective communication!

What criteria will my tutor use?

You will probably have the marking scheme provided in your lab handbook or assignment instructions. Below is an example of a 'typical' lab report marking guide for tutors, but remember that your course marking scheme is unlikely to be exactly the same as this.

Typical marking scheme

Section	To achieve a good mark you need to:	Typical distribution of marks for short lab report
Abstract	• state clear and concise aims • describe the method used • provide a clear description of the results (quantitative comment) • draw conclusions to explain the significance	10
Introduction	• provide sufficient background information • include theoretical informaton in which the experiment is grounded • make references to published literature	15
Method/ Experimental	• give a clear description of the steps taken in an appropriate style • provide sufficient information for the experiment to be replicated • (if appropriate) provide clear, labelled diagrams of apparatus and/or experimental set-up	10
Results	• present and describe results clearly • use appropriate tables and figures, correctly labelled • include appropriate units • (if appropriate) include core calculations	15

Section	To achieve a good mark you need to:	Typical distribution of marks for short lab report
Discussion	• assess and explain results (with reference to literature and theory) • discuss the significance of results • compare your results to published or theoretical values • explain any errors • link back to aims	15
Conclusions	• summarise your main results and the discussion to show the significance and achievement of aims	10
References	• include accurate in-text citations and final reference list	5
Presentation	• present work to a professional standard • write clearly so that the message is easy to follow • avoid spelling or grammar mistakes • keep to the word count • provide a correct balance of length in all sections • use technical terms appropriately and accurately • follow the scientific writing style accurately	20

1 Use the criteria above to do a self-assessment of your strengths and weaknesses.

> **Theory** A formal rule (or set of rules) or idea(s) devised to explain a fact, an event, a phenomenon or occurrence or used to rationalise and support an opinion or explanation.

   a Identify areas that you feel confident about and areas that you will need to take extra care in to get a good mark.

   b For the areas you feel less confident about, think about an action plan to help you feel better equipped to succeed.

Your action plan may look like this:

What I feel confident about (and why)	What I am worried about (and why, and what I will do about it)
Presenting figures clearly and appropriately in the Results section. I am usually good at making my work look professional, and using visuals to support complex ideas.	Including the right amount of theory in the Introduction. I will: • Read lecture notes and lab manual to understand the theory. • Make notes on the main points of the theory. • Write a first draft, explaining the key points. • Edit to ensure it is written concisely and clearly, and includes reference to my reading sources.

2   Once you have written your first draft of your lab report, use
     the criteria above *and* the specific criteria given to you by the
     department to check that you have fulifIled them.

Other factors that your tutor will consider

If this is not your first assignment, you may have already received feedback on previous work. Your tutor will want to see that you have taken
comments into account and made improvements.

Make sure you:

- read previous feedback carefully before you start writing;

- make notes of the areas/points highlighted as needing
  improvement;

- write your lab report with these points in mind;

- use your notes when you have finished writing to check that you
  have not made errors in the areas highlighted.

Using feedback to make improvements

How would you respond to the following feedback from your tutor? Jot down some steps you would take to ensure that you didn't make the same mistake again.

> The lab report showed understanding of the science, but marks were lost for not following standard layout and organisation.

Steps taken

....

> Poor use of punctuation and grammar let the lab report down.

Steps taken

....

> There were no references to the literature anywhere.

Steps taken

....

In your next lab report, make sure you include information about sources of error in your Discussion section, NOT the Results section.

Steps taken

....

The Method section was written in a non-academic style, with personal pronouns throughout.

Steps taken

....

Figures were just plonked in with no reference to them in the text.

Steps taken

....

CHECK POINT Are you ready to submit?

Are you confident that you understand what you are being assessed on?

Try the following checks before you submit your work.

		Yes or No?	Notes
1	Have you looked at your marking criteria carefully?		
2	Do you understand what you are being assessed on for each criteria?		
3	Have you tried writing your lab report with the criteria to hand to check you are doing the right thing?		
4	Have you ticked off each of the criteria when you feel you have achieved these?		

How can I check I have done a good job?

10 second summary

Finally, you will be given tips to help you edit and proof read your work to ensure you submit the best piece of writing you can.

60 second summary

Editing and proof reading

Not even the best writers produce perfect writing straight away. We all make mistakes that we don't notice immediately, or find that we haven't said exactly what we wanted to say. Good writing only comes about as the end product of a staged process. The final stages of this process are the editing and proof-reading.

Once you feel you have finished your 'first draft' – the first version of the finished lab report – you need to step away from your work, and allow some time to let your lab report rest.

It can be hard to notice how clear your writing is, and spot errors such as typos, grammar mistakes and inaccurate punctuation, so we need to do our editing and proof reading with fresh eyes.

Follow these tips to ensure your final product is as good as it can possibly be!

> Writing is a process – you will tweak, bend, twist and shape your work to make a final product that is all yours.

Important first tip

Editing and proof reading are not a 'quick fix'. You need time to do a good job so you must work backwards from the submission deadline and allow yourself a few days for checking your work. If you think of the deadline as just for completing your first draft, you will not be submitting the 'best possible work'.

What's the difference between editing and proof reading?

The first job is editing. This is where you check that you have said what you intended to say, and that you have said it as clearly as possible. You also need to check that you have done what you were asked to do! Of course, you will do some proof reading whilst you are editing – if you spot a spelling mistake, you will correct it!

Proof reading is the final stage, when you read through your completed draft to check for errors with spelling, grammar or punctuation. Proof reading is checking for *accuracy*.

A student
told us

'I find it really hard to notice my own mistakes.'

How do I edit my lab report?

The first check you should do is to look at the instructions again.

- Are you sure you have addressed the task correctly?

- Read the marking criteria to ensure you are absolutely clear about what your tutor wants.

Now you are ready to start the editing process. Follow these steps to ensure you have checked your work thoroughly:

The editing stairway: five steps to your final lab report

Start at the bottom step and move up the stairway.

Step 5: Check for clarity
Have you structured each section logically?
Does your writing flow within and between paragraphs?
Is it easy to read? Are any of your sentences too
long/not clear?

Step 4: Check your scientific writing
Have you followed scientific writing rules and conventions with
layout, abbreviations, tables and figures, and objective style?
Have you used formal language?

Step 3: Check your sources and examples
Have you included enough different sources to give evidence to your
background information? Are your examples clear? Are your references
accurately cited? Have you used your own words?

Step 2: Check the content
Read to check that you have included everything you need to have included
Remove anything that is not directly relevant

**Step 1: Review your work in sections (have you got the right
sections in the right order?)**
Follow the next steps for each section

Do some editing and proof reading

Can you find any mistakes in this extract from the Introduction section of a lab report? Use steps 2 to 5 in the editing stairway, and try to find one mistake for each step (no need to use step 1, as this is not the whole lab report).

Material testing is really important for engineers – generating experimental data for a given material's precise response under load allows it to be modelled accurately during the design phase, and crucially, prevents catastrophic failure of a design. In many cases, the consequence of a product failing unexpectedly could be serious injury or death – it is absolutely essential that engineers know not only when a material will fail, but also begin to plastically deform as in many cases this can lead to overall failure of a design. An example of the kind of failure possible is shown in figure 1, where sections of a steel construction have buckled.

Mistakes with:

Step 2 Some repetition of ideas. E.g. ... *prevents catastrophic failure of a design* ..., and ... *and can lead to overall failure of a design.* The second example can be deleted (see final improved version below).

Step 3 One or two sources should be included. E.g. the first sentence could have a reference.

Step 4 Informal language in sentence 1: *really important*. Replace with '*critical*'. Also, figure needs a capital 'F': ...is shown in Figure 1 ...

Step 5 Sentence 1 is unnecessarily long and a bit unclear. Rewrite something like this: Material testing is critical for engineers. The experimental data generated for a given material's precise response under load can be used in the design phase and crucially, prevent catastrophic failure of a design.

Improved version:

Material testing is critical for engineers. The experimental data generated for a given material's precise response under load can be used in the design phase and crucially, prevent catastrophic failure of a design(1). In many cases, the consequence of a product failing unexpectedly could be serious injury or death, and thus, it is absolutely essential that engineers know not only when a material will fail, but also begin to plastically deform. An example of the kind of failure possible is shown in Figure 1, where sections of a steel construction have buckled(2).

How do I proof read?

Once all the editing work has been done, it's time to do the final check for typos. This involves careful, quite slow, reading. You need to check for the following:

- Is every word you need included (you may be surprised by how often we leave out 'small' words, because our brain assumes they are there)?

- Are any words not needed?

- Is every word written correctly (spelling, and no 'contractions')?

- Are your sentences punctuated accurately?

Tip!

Read your work aloud to work out where you take natural pauses. This will indicate the need for commas or even full stops. It will also flag up faulty punctuation – where you have put a comma, but actually there is no need for one.

CHECK
POINT
Final checks

Just before you submit your work, you should do one final check.

Ask yourself these questions:

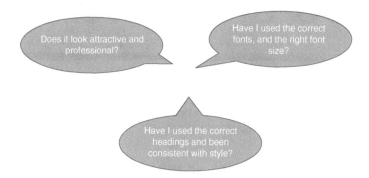

Does it look attractive and professional?

Have I used the correct fonts, and the right font size?

Have I used the correct headings and been consistent with style?

You can now submit your work!

Final checklist: How to know you are done

To be absolutely sure you know how to write a good lab report, work through this final checklist.

1 Do you know what the reader wants to learn from your lab report and why they need to know? ❏

2 Do you know what sections you need to include in your lab report and what to include in each section? ❏

3 Do you know the different possible variations in lab reports from different subjects? ❏

4 Are you clear about the different steps you need to go through before, during and after writing your lab report? ❏

5 Do you know what style of writing you need to use in your lab report? ❏

6   Have you understood the rules about using tables
    and figures?   ☐

7   Do you know when and how to cite the sources
    you have read?   ☐

8   Are you clear about the relative lengths of the different
    sections of the lab report?   ☐

9   Do you know how you will be assessed?   ☐

10 Are you confident you can edit and check your work?   ☐

Now you are ready to write great lab reports!

Glossary

Abbreviation   A short form of a word or phrase used to replace the long form.

Abstract   A brief summary (typically 150–250 words) of a research study which includes aims, methods used, results and overall conclusions.

Apparatus   The technical and/or laboratory equipment used to conduct an activity or experiment.

Appendix (Appendices)   A separate section at the end of a lab report (or any book or document) that provides additional information.

Citation   A quote from or reference to an academic or other formal text using a particular referencing system such as Harvard (name, date) or Vancouver (numeric).

Figure   A picture, diagram or drawing, often numbered, found in academic texts such as lab reports and used to describe (often) complex information in a visual way.

Lab report   A description and analysis of a laboratory experiment that investigates a scientific concept to facilitate scientific research.

Literature Published books, journals and other academic texts on a specific subject or topic.

Objective style Fact / evidence-based and unbiased presentation of information and ideas (usually avoiding the use of personal pronouns like 'I' or 'we').

Paper An academic article, but also sometimes can refer to a presentation delivered at a conference or symposium, and later written up for publication.

Passive construction A type of grammar construction that describes 'what was done' rather than 'who did it'. In the case of scientific writing, for example, the experiment is more important than the experimenter.

References The list of sources of information (from a textbook, an academic article etc.) used in academic work.

Referencing A particular system such as Harvard, APA or Vancouver to refer to a source in academic work, which includes information that tells the reader where the source came from.

Summary An alternative term for Abstract (e.g. in engineering lab reports).

Table A set of facts or figures arranged systematically and usually displayed in rows and columns, often numbered, and found in academic texts such as lab reports and used to describe (often) complex information in a visual way.

Technical report A research document that describes the process, progress, or results of technical or scientific study or analysis of a research problem. A technical report is typically longer and more in depth than a lab report.

Theory A formal rule (or set of rules) or idea(s) devised to explain a fact, an event, a phenomenon or occurrence or used to rationalise and support an opinion or explanation.

Further reading and resources

Field, A. and Hole, G. (2003) *How to Design and Report Experiments*. London: Sage

Provides systematic information about how to plan your research and carry out experiments and gives detailed guidance on the use of statistics. Aimed mostly at students in psychology social science.

Hopkins, D. and Reid, T. (2018) *The Academic Skills Handbook: Your Guide to Success in Writing, Thinking and Communicating at University*. London: Sage.

Our all-in-one Academic Skills toolkit gives you an annotated lab report and an extended chapter on Getting Started on your Lab Report with further guidance, tips and tasks.

Walliman, N. (2019) *Your Research Project: Designing, Planning, and Getting Started*. London: Sage

This book provides guidance on bigger, longer research projects and will take you through from brainstorming and devising research questions to the final written project report.